the Institute of Management
F O U N D A T I O N

The Institute of Management (IM) is at the forefront of management development and best management practice. The Institute embraces all levels of management from students to chief executives. It provides a unique portfolio of services for all managers, enabling them to develop skills and achieve management excellence.

For information on the benefits of membership, please contact:

Department HS
Institute of Management
Cottingham Road
Corby
Northants NN17 1TT

Tel. 01536 204222
Fax 01536 201651

This series is commissioned by the Institute of Management Foundation.

C O N T E N T S

Successful
Meetings
in a week

John and Shirley Payne

ead... ighton

British Library Cataloguing in Publication Data

A catalogue for this title is available from the
British Library

ISBN 0 340 60894 3

First published 1994
Impression number   10   9   8   7   6   5   4   3   2
Year   1999   1998   1997   1996

Typeset by Multiplex Techniques Ltd.
Printed for Hodder & Stoughton Educational, a division of
Hodder Headline Plc, 338 Euston Road, London NW1 3BH by
Redwood Books Ltd, Trowbridge, Wiltshire.

Running a meeting is not most people's idea of fun!

How often have you heard (or used) phrases such as:

- 'What a waste of time that was'
- 'Meetings just never seem to achieve anything'
- 'What should have taken 30 minutes took four hours'
- 'There was just no control at all'
- 'Why did they invite me? I was BORED!'

How is it that some people seem able to run very effective meetings when others in a similar situation simply do not?

Simply by following a few straightforward steps, meetings can be made more effective. They can actually be fun to run (and to attend!).

These steps are:

- decide whether you really need a meeting
- prepare thoroughly
  - purpose, objectives, attendees
  - agenda, venue, room, equipment
- notify the participants in good time
- structure the meeting properly
- control the input effectively
- ensure that results are achieved
- follow up on progress

Preparation: reasons, purpose, objectives and attendees

Today, we will cover the first two steps outlined in the Introduction

- the need for a meeting
- the first part of the Preparation: purpose, objectives, and attendees

Do we need a meeting?

Please think about the meetings you attend or run:

- How many hours per week do you currently spend in meetings?
- What percentage of that time is *effective*?

Answers to these questions will obviously depend on your own situation but fairly typical responses are:

- about eight hours per week
- 25 per cent, if that!

For that person there is the potential to gain *six hours per week*.

Some people seem to believe that the *only* way to communicate with a group of people is via a meeting.

Have you ever sat in a meeting that became a conversation between two people that could easily have been handled over the telephone? So maybe you needed to know the outcome, but that could have been handled by another phone call or a memo, without the need to keep people sitting there for an hour and a half.

Sadly, some meetings become 'institutions' and the justification goes something like: 'Well, there wasn't anything to discuss, but it's Monday and we always have a departmental meeting on Mondays!'

So, on this occasion, maybe ten people including the manager sat there with nothing significant to discuss and wondered why they were all there. Consequently, people probably invented issues just to have something to discuss (like the flavour of the coffee in the coffee machines!). How would you have felt?

Rule one: Do not hold a meeting unless there is a *clear, result-oriented objective*!

Why are some meetings so ineffective?
There can be many reasons but, applying the 80/20 Rule, 20 per cent of those reasons seem to produce 80 per cent of the problems:

- insufficient or no prior notification: 'What meeting?'
- failure to communicate the purpose of the meeting: 'Why are we having this meeting?'
- lack of an effective agenda: 'What are we discussing then?'
- latecomers causing backtracking: 'That's put us back half an hour!'
- lack of any planned finish time: 'How long will this take? I've got another meeting this afternoon'
- poor control of structure by the chair: 'Shouldn't we have discussed this before making that last decision?'
- failure of the chair to control the participants properly:'It became the usual row between Sales and Production. Useless meeting!'
- no sense of achieving anything specific: 'We "discussed" it to death and decided nothing!'
- senior people making control difficult for the chair: 'I wish my Managing Director wouldn't just come into our meeting and simply take over!'

When is a meeting justified?
It might be helpful to define what is meant by a 'meeting' in the context of this book. It is:

> an exchange of information, ideas, or opinions between two or more people with active roles, in order to achieve specific results.

So we are not talking about conferences with 200 people, where each delegate is unlikely to have an active role to play.

Some valid reasons for holding a meeting might be to:

- make a decision
- plan or review progress
- solve problems
- communicate information and allow for clarification
- check reactions prior to making changes
- motivate

You can probably think of others from your own situation.

Preparation, I: Purpose, objectives, attendees

'Failing to prepare is preparing to fail' is an old but very true saying. Inadequate preparation is a major cause of failure in meetings. The problem is that preparation takes time, and time is something that is usually on a tight budget, to say the least!

Some managers say something like: 'I was too busy to prepare for a meeting that I can easily run "off the cuff".' They should try asking the other attendees how *they* felt!

If a meeting is going to be effective, we have to *make* the time for preparation. It may take 20 minutes to prepare a proper agenda before the meeting but that is better than unnecessarily wasting two hours for each of eight people.

To recap, the following are the basic steps in preparation for a meeting:

- decide the purpose and objectives of the meeting
- select the attendees
- produce an agenda
- select the venue
- organise the room and equipment
- send out the agenda in sufficient time

Today, we will deal with the first two of these steps.

The purpose of the meeting
In this step, two questions need to be answered:

- Why is this meeting needed?
- Is a meeting the best way to achieve that purpose?

Look back to the earlier section on 'When is a meeting justified?' Identify the purpose as specifically as you can at this stage.

For example:

> • to select a new computer
> • to review progress on a project
> • to inform people of a revised accounting system
> • to agree targets for the next month

There may well be several reasons for holding the same meeting. It is important to be realistic here. Don't attempt to do too much in any one meeting.

Now, decide whether a meeting is the best way of achieving that purpose.

For example, if the revised accounting system mentioned above only requires the team to know about a few minor straightforward changes then why not summarise them on one sheet of paper and send it out, rather than meet?

The objectives of the meeting
A well-stated objective should be:

> • clear
> • realistic
> • measurable, wherever possible
> • should show the *result*, the *deadline* and any constraints

The importance of result-oriented objectives for meetings cannot be overstressed; sadly, they are often lacking. The frequent complaint 'That meeting didn't achieve anything' can often be traced back to a lack of clear objectives.

Thinking outside the work situation, we wouldn't spend vast sums of money on simply 'buying a house'. There's more to it than that. We would probably think or say something like: 'By the end of next month, we need to choose a house with at least three bedrooms and costing no more than £****'.

In the context of meetings, this is the difference between

Discuss Project 'X'

and

By the end of this meeting we will have reviewed progress on Project 'X', identified any potential problems, decided *what actions* are necessary, agreed *who* will carry them out, and *by when*.

The second is much clearer but takes some time to think out. We are convinced that time is worth it!

There may well be several objectives to be achieved within the same meeting. Rarely does a meeting have only one.

The attendees
Now that the objectives are clear, it is possible to decide who needs to attend the meeting to ensure achievement of those objectives.

Everyone should have a reason to be there and, if possible, have an active role to play. This 'active role' can be hard to define, so an example might help.

Suppose we are trying to decide who is needed to achieve the 'Project X' objective above. The team leader will certainly need to be there, together possibly with team members who have something to contribute. These people will have an active role. It may also help to invite a new team leader who will learn from the meeting. There is a valid reason for that person to be there even though they will probably not have an active role.

It is vital that each person understands why they are there and what they are expected to contribute. The manager might know the reason. That does *not* mean that the attendee knows it!

When selecting the attendees, watch out for three 'traps' for the unwary:

- beware of 'stand-ins'
- beware of a senior manager 'take-over'
- beware of 'status invitations'

Beware of 'stand-ins': Some decision-making meetings have been ruined by the attendance (without any warning) of 'stand-ins' who have not been given any authority by their boss. This puts them in a difficult situation as they only feel able to listen and report back, and the others at the meeting become frustrated because no decisions are made.

The stand-in rule: In the case of decision-making meetings, no stand-ins are allowed unless they have the necessary *authority to decide.*

If the attendee cannot attend and is not prepared to delegate authority – postpone the meeting!

If the meeting cannot be postponed, let them know that a decision must be made, and why.

They then have three choices:

- to accept a decision made in their absence
- to send a stand-in with authority
- to rearrange things so they can attend

Beware when inviting senior managers. No, we are not anti-senior management! Their presence poses a problem for even the most effective 'chair'.

Some people invite them to add weight to a meeting: 'If the boss is going to be there it must be important'. This may be true, and it is also valid where senior management authority is required for a particular decision.

The problem is that sometimes they tend to take over! Most senior managers are used to running meetings and quite naturally fall into the role of 'chair'. This is compounded by the fact that people often tend to address comments and questions to the most senior person there.

These problems can be handled in advance and will be covered in the section on 'Handling more senior people' on Friday.

For now, just be aware of the risks as well as the benefits.

Beware of 'status invites'. This trap goes something like: 'I'm inviting the Head of Section A so I had better invite the

Heads of the other three sections as well in case they get upset about being left out'.

Few of us enjoy upsetting others, but there is a possibly false assumption here. Unless the issue is of concern to them, they may *welcome* being 'left out' rather than spend two hours sitting in a (for them) pointless meeting, they may well prefer to do something more productive!

Try *asking* them before finalising the list of attendees. We know that this sounds obvious, but often it simply is not done. When was the last time you were asked if you *wanted* to attend a meeting?

From past experience, the reply is often: 'Thanks. No, I really don't need to be there, but I would like to know the final decision you make please'.

Summary

Preparation
- purpose: is a meeting the *best* way of meeting the objective?
- objectives: result-oriented, clear, measurable and realistic
- make time to prepare
- attendees: need a reason to be there, beware of stand-ins, deal in advance with potential problems with senior manager attendees

Preparation: setting up the meeting

Yesterday, we covered the need for a meeting and the first part of preparation. Today we will cover the second part of preparation:

- producing an effective agenda
- selecting the venue
- booking the meeting room and equipment
- notifying the participants

Producing an effective agenda

Most people recognise the need for an agenda to provide some structure for the meeting, but, in addition to helping the 'chair' to keep control, the agenda should help the participants to *prepare* for the meeting.

Let's start by looking at a fairly typical agenda.

A typical agenda

Date: 15th August

Place: Head Office, Room 3

Time: 10 a.m.

Attendees: PBR, MAV, RT, MS, DL

Items to be covered:

1   Minutes of last meeting

2   Project 'X'

3   Budgets

4   New computer

5   Any other business

6   Date for next meeting

This provides a sequence for the 'chair' and tells the participants what topics will be covered.

Before reading any further, put yourself in the role of a potential attendee and consider how you would react to an agenda such as this.

Some fairly typical reactions might be:

- 'I'm not involved with Project 'X' so why should I sit through this part?'
- 'Is that the budgets for *this* year or *next* year?'
- 'Are we deciding *which* computer or has someone already done that?'
- 'I hope we don't spend half an hour discussing the flavour of the coffee in "Any Other Business" again'
- 'When will the meeting finish?'
- 'What is the meeting trying to achieve?'

In short, it is unclear. As an aid to preparation by participants, it is *useless*!

An effective agenda should:

- show specific objectives rather than topics
- show an estimated finish time as well as a start time
- show who is involved in meeting each objective
- if possible, allow people to attend only those items that are relevant to them

Using the general 'topic'-based agenda from the previous page as a basis, here is an example of an agenda that meets the criteria for an effective agenda:

A suggested agenda format

Date: 15th August l994   **Place:** Head Office, Room 3

Start time: 10 a.m. (*sharp please!*) **Finish time:** 12 noon

Attendees: Peter Rawlings (chair), David Leeds (scribe), Mark South, Madge Vanion, Dennis Thomas

Item No.	Objective	Who	Time
	By the end of this meeting, we will have:		
1.	Reviewed progress on the actions we agreed at the last meeting	PR	15 mins
2.	Discussed individual requirements, and produced a department budget for next year	All	1 hr
3.	Decided which additional personal computer to buy for the department (information on the three options is attached)	All	15 mins
4.	Reviewed progress on Project 'X', identified actions needed, who will act, and by when	MS	30 mins

If any important issues arise between now and the date of the meeting, please let me know and I will revise the agenda.

Attendance vital:

Objectives 1–3: everyone

Objective 4: Peter + Mark and David (project team)

Again, think how you, as a potential participant, would react to this agenda. Would it help your preparation? How would you feel about attending the meeting? How would you expect the meeting to run?

Now think about it from the viewpoint of the 'chair'. Would it alter the conduct of the meeting? Is anything likely to be harder or easier?

Some of the items included in this agenda are self-explanatory, so we will concentrate on those aspects that are worth explanation.

1 Starting time

How many meetings do you attend (or run) that actually *start* on time? Most meeting have an official 'start time' but very few meetings actually start at that time. Fifteen or 30 minutes late is not unusual – but look at the cost of wasted

time, to say nothing of simple bad manners. Often the participants are sitting there waiting for the last member and simply do not know when, or even if, he or she will arrive. People quickly learn whether a particular meeting/ chair always starts on time.

As you will see from the sample agenda, (*sharp please!*) has been put after the start time. If you use it, you must *do* it.

(NB: Some ideas for handling latecomers will be covered on Thursday.)

2 Objectives
As discussed earlier, list the objectives that you have already set. As these show the *specific results* rather than simply ill-defined topics, preparation by the participants is likely to be more effective. Specific objectives also make it easier for the chair to estimate the time needed to achieve the result. The sequence of objectives will be important if decisions made under one objective will affect another objective. See also the notes under 'Time' below.

3 Time
This is one of the trickiest areas in the agenda if you have never tried to do this before. As with any form of estimating, the more you do it, the better you get. Consider two factors: the *importance* of the objective and its urgency. An objective that is both important and urgent should be dealt with early and given adequate time, whereas an item that is relatively unimportant but very urgent might be dealt with at the start but given 10 minutes maximum.

Think about each objective. Consider how much time it is worth, then, in the early days of estimating times, add a bit of 'cover' to reduce the chances of any overrun. If you don't use the 'cover' time, *no one objects to a meeting that finishes early*.

4 *Who is involved*

The column headed 'Who' shows *the person primarily responsible for that particular objective*, e.g. the project leader of a particular project on this agenda. They may well involve others in the project group, but that is up to them. The first time you use this, explain what the initials mean.

5 *Preparatory reading*

Have you ever had to spend time in a meeting reading through material prior to any discussion? This can be a big time-waster and so often it is unnecessary. Where possible, send out documentation with the agenda. People can then fit the reading in at a time convenient to them. An example of this approach has been used with the 'computer' objective (no.3) in the sample agenda.

This thinking can also be applied to meetings where the minutes of the last meeting are read and approved, unless there is concern about confidentiality or sensitivity.

6 Any other business (AOB)
You will have spotted that this has been dropped.

A plea from the heart – *please do not use this.*

AOB is usually used to allow discussion of items suggested by the participants (rather than the chair). The problem is that no preparation can be done for these items and often a disproportionate amount of time is given by the meeting to a minor concern from one person, that could have been more effectively handled outside the meeting.

There is an alternative that is more effective. Before preparing the agenda, explain that there is no 'AOB' and ask the participants to give you any objectives that they would like achieved at the meeting. If these are valid business for the meeting then include them in the agenda; if not, discuss them with the person concerned to decide how best to resolve the issue. People soon become used to this way of working, and seem to like it. (Handling emergency items which were not on the original agenda will be covered on Tuesday.)

7 'Attendance vital'
Have you ever sat through a fairly lengthy discussion in a meeting thinking: 'This item is nothing to do with me. I'm not involved and it has no effect on my unit?'

If it is not feasible to set up separate meetings then consider the following idea: *Allow (even encourage) people to come and go.*

You will see from the sample agenda that the last item is project-related and concerns only the project team, so why should the others have to stay?

It will not always be possible to put this type of item at the end, so let's look at another situation where the item has to be dealt with first. As time for each item is estimated, the remaining participants know when to come in.

Most 'chairs' when they first see this think: 'Sorry, it won't work! People will forget or come late', etc. All that we can say is that 99 per cent *don't*! People seem to play fair. It is saving their time and they genuinely seem to appreciate it. To avoid a situation where someone might feel excluded even though the issue may not directly affect them, try asking them beforehand if they want to attend that section of the meeting.

While this type of agenda is much clearer, it is only fair to say that it takes much longer to prepare. A 'topics'-based agenda would probably take five minutes to produce, whereas this 'objectives'-based agenda will take perhaps 20 minutes to draw up. Having used this approach for a long time now, we can assure you that the extra 15 minutes is more than worth it!

Selecting the venue

Choosing the venue for a meeting is often something that, sadly, receives little attention. There also seems to be an unwritten law that states 'the location will always be that of the most senior attendee'.

Consider:

- the location of all participants, and decide where the most appropriate location would be to minimise travel time or costs, and inconvenience
- whether the meeting objectives will be helped by actually *seeing* a particular building, room, piece of equipment, etc. – but consider the use of photos or videos if more appropriate
- whether the meeting might need to have access to a specific computer, or a set of files that cannot easily be transported

Booking the meeting room and equipment

Booking the meeting room
The room needs to be adequate for the number of
participants in terms of:

- layout and size
- lighting, heating and ventilation

The layout and size of the room are governed not only by
the number of participants, but also by the amount of
involvement required from each to meet the objectives set
for the meeting effectively.

There are three basic layouts:

- 'cinema' style – useful primarily for conferences
  where a large number of people are listening to one
  or more presentations with minimal individual
  involvement. With this layout there is little or no
  space for paperwork
- 'U' or 'V shape – for groups up to a maximum of 20
  where the focus needs to be towards the front, e.g.
  for a presentation or two using visual aids, but with
  more opportunity for individual involvement and
  cross-table discussion
- 'boardroom' style, where everyone sits round a large
  table – suitable usually for smaller meetings.
  Promotes cross-table discussion. Use of visual aids
  is often difficult with this layout as the view can be
  blocked by others

The seats should be comfortable enough for the duration of the meeting. On an uncomfortable chair, even one hour can seem like a lifetime.

If people need to read documents and/or make notes, good lighting is essential, otherwise there are too many side conversations as people ask each other: 'Can *you* see what this says?' If projectors are to be used, it helps if the area around the screen can be dimmed, to make the image clearer for everyone.

The temperature needs to be reasonable for the participants. This sounds obvious, but often the chair/presenters are more active so do not feel as cold as the participants sitting quietly. Nerves generate central heating!

A note on smoking: Smoking is banned at many meetings nowadays. If in doubt, ask the attendees whether anyone objects to smoking in the meeting. If so, most people would accept a 'ban'. If smoking *is* allowed by the group, *please* ensure that the room is adequately ventilated. Better still, allow a smoking break every 45 minutes or so when the

smokers can 'have a puff' in another area (over a coffee, perhaps?). Tell the smokers what facilities there are for them; don't let them sit and wonder.

Booking the equipment
A little cautionary tale: Jean, a manager in Company A, was invited to Company B to give a presentation. She duly arrived with a superb set of overhead slides, only to find that the only equipment available was a flip chart. She should have checked, perhaps; but in Company B, presentations were always made with prepared flips and no one had told her what Company B's practice was.

If people are asked to give a presentation, either tell them what equipment is available, or find out what they require.

On Friday, we will look at how to control input and ensure a clear result from the meeting. A flip chart is of great help here, so if at all possible try to have one in the room. Some people feel that a flip chart is rather 'schoolteacherish', but it has real advantages for both clarification and for control, and people recognise that. Just put up with the jokes.

Notifying the participants

It's not much fun to arrive at a meeting to find the agenda on the table and realise that you do not have the necessary information with you. The agenda is vital for participants' preparation, so it must go out in sufficient time to allow for that preparation. If the meeting is to meet only the objectives set by the chair then five days is probably sufficient preparation time, assuming that the date had been booked earlier.

If, however, you want to include other objectives that previously would have been brought up by the participants and covered in 'Any Other Business', then send out a *draft* agenda about 10 days before, with a request for any other objectives from participants. The *final* agenda then goes out around five days before the meeting as usual.

Summary

Agenda
- ensure that the agenda
  - shows the objectives
  - shows a start and finish time
  - avoids 'Any Other Business'

Venue
- when selecting the venue, consider the location of the attendees, and the need for access to data

The room
- layout: cinema, 'U' or 'V' shape, or boardroom
- adequate heating and ventilation

The equipment
- find out what is needed or inform them

The participants
- ensure they receive the agenda in time to prepare

1572

Structure: general guidelines

Today we will cover the first four aspects of structuring the meeting:

- opening the meeting
- introducing each agenda item
- explaining the roles
- setting the ground rules

I'M SURE NONE OF US WOULD WANT TO BE TOO RIGID AND STRUCTURED IN APPROACH...

If you don't know where you are going, you are likely to end up somewhere else! The objectives for the meeting tell you 'where you are going'; an effective structure should help you ensure that you don't 'end up somewhere else'. Unfortunately, some 'chairs' simply do not appear to have any structure in their meetings. Have you ever sat there and thought, 'Where is this going?' This lack of structure may be because the chair doesn't know how to provide one; or they may purposely avoid it because they see it as a potential 'straitjacket', preventing creativity.

Today we will cover how to provide some general structure; tomorrow, we will look at how to structure various types of meeting, including those that need creativity.

Opening the meeting

Various research projects in the past have shown pretty conclusively that people tend to form impressions very quickly, in a matter of a couple of minutes. So the introduction is important because it seems to 'set the tone' for the rest of the meeting.

The introduction should welcome the participants and review the agenda.

Welcome the participants
Start by thanking the people for their attendance and (if they have!) for arriving on time to enable a prompt start. Review the overall purpose of the meeting and check that everyone there actually *received* the agenda. Just because they are there does not mean they have the agenda; they might have noted the date and time when attending a previous meeting.

Review the agenda
This overall review is to check for any concerns. Most of the time, there will not be any; the group will be happy with the agenda as it stands, and you will be able to go straight to the first objective and get started.

However, the agenda was probably sent out a few days ago. The purpose of this review is to check whether there are any important and/or urgent issues (unknown to you) that have arisen during this period, or even emergencies immediately prior to the meeting. For example, one of the participants has just received a major complaint over the phone from your largest customer that calls for some immediate decisions. You can't just ignore it, so what do you do?

Handling 'emergency' items not on the original agenda

The first question has to be: 'Is it relevant to the meeting?' Assuming that it *is* relevant, then the objectives or agenda will have to be revised.

Depending on the situation, you probably have two alternatives: drop one or more of the agenda items, or extend the duration of the meeting.

1   Drop one or more of the agenda items.   If the 'emergency' item is both urgent and important but the participants *must* leave at the stated finish time, you have little choice but to postpone the least important/urgent items(s).

Explain the problem, and ask for participants' suggestions on which item to drop. In circumstances like this they will understand (because the issue is relevant to them as well) and will usually be more than helpful in re-prioritising.

2   Extend the duration of the meeting.   Let's take the worst case. The new issue is urgent and important, any 'contingency' time you have built in to the timings will not be sufficient to cope with the emergency, and the existing objectives for the meeting must be achieved today. The duration has to be extended!

If you explain the situation (including the consequences of not acting) and involve the participants, they are likely to arrive at the same conclusion. Ask for their views, and agree a revised finish time. This is usually feasible: few people make appointments which *immediately* follow a meeting, so there is usually some room to manoeuvre. Some people will be happy to stay later providing they can make a quick phone call. Make the facility available there and then, otherwise it will only be 'on their mind' until they make the call.

If most can stay but one or two have to leave at the original time, see if you can reorder the sequence of agenda items so that they can still leave. Under *genuine* crisis conditions, you might be surprised just how cooperative people can be.

Make the objectives visible
Your A4 agenda with the objectives clearly stated is fine –
for preparation. During the meeting it is very easy for it to
get buried under papers or files. We have derived
considerable benefit from putting the objectives and finish
time on a previously prepared flip chart in a position where
all can see it. This way the objectives are permanently visible
and provide a reminder of the expected results, timings and
sequence which helps with control generally.

Introducing each agenda item

When introducing each agenda item, the following points
should be covered:

- clarify the objective
- explain any background

Clarify the objective
Ensure that everyone is clear about the *expected result*. It is
also helpful just to check at this point that any necessary
preparation has been done.

Explain any background
Explain briefly why this objective has arisen, together with
its importance and urgency.

Explaining the roles

It is important to be clear about the roles to be played by the
'chair', participants, and 'scribe', where appropriate.

Role of the chair
We see the role of the chair as controlling the conduct of the meeting so that the planned results (the objectives) are achieved.

One difficulty that faces most 'chairs' at some point is deciding whether you should be participating or chairing. Occasionally, the 'chair' may be the most knowledgeable person on a particular topic and it is hard to chair when you are doing the bulk of the talking. You might be rambling on a bit and not even recognise it.

Suppose you decide that you should really become a participant for that agenda item because you are the one with all the information. What should you do? Consider using a *stand-in 'chair'* for that item.

Many years ago, I worked for a boss who was a 'production expert'. I was usually 'scribe' in his meetings. If he had a 'production' item on the agenda in which he needed significant involvement, he would tell me beforehand that he would hand over to me.

You might be thinking, 'How on earth do you tell your own boss to shut up?' Easy! You agree that 'ground rule' (in private). He actually used to make a joke of it. 'John will enjoy telling me to shut up if need be.' And I did!

He never argued once when I 'controlled', but I did know what he was trying to achieve. That was part of our prior discussion as well.

A second major task is deciding how much involvement is needed. As we noted above, the 'chair' has to control the conduct of the meeting to ensure that the results are achieved. This invariably means deciding how much involvement by the participants is appropriate. If you ever had the misfortune to attend an important meeting that lacked any sort of control by the 'chair', or where too much or too little involvement was allowed, you will know exactly why it is so important.

Not surprisingly, most people 'chair' using their own natural approach – so, if you are naturally a fairly democratic person, then you will probably encourage a fairly high level of involvement.

The difficulty is that no single approach is likely to suit every situation. (Try being democratic at a road accident!) Our natural approach may be fine for most chairing situations but there will be occasions when we have to behave differently, that is, use more or less involvement than we might do naturally.

There appears to be a strong link between *involvement* and *commitment*: i.e. the more involvement, the greater the commitment. However, it is a mistake to assume that the *only* way to get commitment is to have involvement. It is not!

If the others know virtually nothing and see you as 'the expert' whom they trust, you will probably get commitment without any involvement. In fact, if you try to involve them, they probably could not answer your questions!

There is another related misconception. Some people *always* try to get commitment because they believe that is what a 'chair' *should* do. Not so. If a policemen decides to give you a speeding ticket, do you really think he is looking for *commitment*?

Sometimes it is unrealistic to try to get commitment; all you can really hope for is *acceptance* and that may well be sufficient. Suppose one item in your meeting concerns some new mandatory company procedure. It is probably unrealistic to expect people to be enthusiastic about it; all that you can really hope for is that they accept it has to be implemented. It must be done – like it or not.

So, it is important that you as 'chair' know clearly how much involvement you need from the participants to enable you to explain their role.

Role of the participants
By 'role' we mean *the expected level of involvement of the participants*.

Few chairs seem actually to explain this, but virtually all consider it. Have you ever attended a meeting where people input their views and proposals only to find (an hour later) that the 'decision' had already been made? The chair had obviously not explained their role. Just ask yourself what effect it had on motivation?

In the previous section on the role of the 'chair', we talked about the need to decide whether acceptance or commitment is needed and how much involvement is required.

The chair should explain what involvement (if any) is needed from the group to meet the objective, and why.

Role of the scribe
We strongly believe that a flip chart is a major aid in meetings. It makes key information visible to all, and keeps the focus 'at the front', which makes control easier.

Most people find it hard to chair and write on a flip chart at the same time, so a good scribe is one of your most important assets.

The scribe is really a second 'chair'. As well as accurately recording key information/decisions, the good ones will help you with control (if you let them).

Warning: never give the job of scribe to an awkward participant to keep him or her quiet!

We know it can be tempting ('This will shut him up for once') but you are giving them *power*. The awkward type might well abuse it! They are invariably standing behind you so you can't easily see what they are doing. Only use someone you can trust to do a good job.

Explain to the scribe that they have the right to interrupt and halt the discussion for clarification, to slow things down, or to check that they have captured the key points. You should also give them the chance to add their views; strangely this is very often forgotten.

Setting the ground rules

'Ground rules' are one of the best ways to prevent problems, during the discussion. Many chairs set them too late (or not at all). If you expect trouble on an agenda item, set 'ground rules' when introducing it.

What do we mean by a 'ground rule?' It is a method of operating, or standard of behaviour, *applied to the whole group*, to help to ensure that the result is achieved.

To illustrate the benefit, suppose that you anticipate that an item will generate a lot of feeling and that it could degenerate into an argument between two or three of the participants. When introducing the item you might say something like: 'I appreciate that this is a fairly emotive item. So that we can all hear the various views, can we please just have one person speaking at a time. Secondly, please ensure that any disagreements are constructive, i.e. give us an alternative. Is that agreed by everyone?' You may well have really used the ground rule to deal with only one or two people but, because it is applied to all when everyone is calm, most people will accept them. Then, if A and B start to argue during the discussions, you can refer back to the ground rule which was agreed at the start.

Summary

Opening the meeting
- welcome and thank
- review agenda, and re-plan any 'emergency' items
- make the objectives visible

Introducing each agenda item
- clarify the objective and explain the background

Explaining the roles
- decide the level of involvement required
- explain what involvement you need from the participants, and why
- explain the role of the scribe, and give authority

Setting the ground rules
- standards of behaviour applicable to everyone
- use ground rules to prevent trouble

Structure: specific situations

Today we will cover five further aspects of structuring the meeting:

- making decisions
- planning or reviewing progress
- solving problems
- communicating information
- checking reactions

RIGHT, WE'VE WEIGHED UP ALL THE PROS AND CONS — WHO'S GOING TO CALL THE TOSS?

Yesterday we suggested some ideas to help the chair in structuring meetings generally. Today we will look at the structure for specific situations.

The participants in the meeting might be crystal clear about the objective, but be rather unsure as to the best way to go about actually achieving it. For example, they know that they need to decide which computer to buy for the department, but are unsure about the best way collectively to make the choice when preferences differ widely.

The following sections provide a suggested structure for each of the situations listed above. Please bear in mind that these ideas are *guidelines*. Compare our ideas with your own approach in each case and use whichever best suits the situations that you have to handle.

Making decisions

Once the chair has made sure that the objective is clear to everyone, they have understood why the decision is needed, and you have verified that any 'stand-in' has the authority to make decisions (see the Sunday chapter), the first question needs to be: 'What *type* of decision are we trying to make?' as this governs the structure.

Types of decision
Basically there are two types which we term 'logical' and 'creative'.

Logical decisions are those where there are a number of pre-set options and the objective is to decide which option best meets the requirements. For example, choosing which computer to buy for the department would probably fall into this category.

Creative decisions are those where there are no pre-set options. Options have first to be created before a choice can be made. For example, deciding the best way to launch a totally new business, where nothing similar has existed before, is a creative decision.

What we will now do is to look at the structure (approach) for both of the situations.

Structure for 'logical' decisions
Start by covering the overall purpose (the objective). Then, to avoid differences of opinion turning into argument, consider asking the group to *identify the criteria*.

For example, when deciding which candidate to recruit from a shortlist, your criteria would probably include experience, qualifications, skills, knowledge, etc. Try to be as specific as possible and, if it helps, break the criteria into two categories, *essential* and *desirable*. Essential criteria are those on which there is no room for manoeuvre, e.g. minimum qualifications. The desirable criteria are 'nice to have', e.g. amount of experience above the minimum. If there are several desirable criteria they are unlikely to be equally important, so consider rating them using either a 'high, medium, low' or a numerical scale.

Try listing the criteria on a flip chart as you go. Keeping the focus on the flip chart at the end of the room reduces (but doesn't eliminate) the chances of cross-table argument. This is where a 'scribe' helps once again. He or she is concentrating on recording the information from the group, whereas the chair can concentrate on keeping control.

Once the criteria have been set, the next stage in the structure is to record (on the flip) the information on each of the options, eliminate any that do not meet any essential criteria, then see which of the options left best meet the criteria.

Before the group finalises the decision it is always worth asking it to make sure that any snags have been identified and considered.

In decision-making, some people see only the benefits, some see only snags, and some take an objective view by considering both. It is up to the chair to ensure that the group makes an objective choice.

Structure for 'logical' decisions
- ensure that the objective is clear and explain why the decision must be made
- identify the criteria and list them on a flip chart
- review the options, record the information and see which option best meets the criteria
- don't forget to consider the snags, as well as the benefits
- chair to ensure an objective decision is made

Structure for 'creative' decisions
By definition, creative decisions need rather more 'free rein' than logical decisions. The aim is to generate possible options, where none (or too few) currently exist.

'Free rein' doesn't mean chaos! Some structure is still needed; it is just different from that used for logical decisions.

Start by covering the purpose: i.e. the objective is to generate possible options then select the most appropriate.

Paradoxically, the creative process is helped by a few 'ground rules'.

1   Explain that the idea is 'quantity', not 'quality', at this point. What is needed is as many options as possible. The quality will be evaluated later in the process.

2   Do not set criteria yet. The existence of criteria seems to limit creativity; the more restrictions, the fewer ideas. Hold this step until later. It is important to ensure that people understand that they should not evaluate any of the ideas proposed, and why.

3   All ideas should be recorded verbatim on a flip chart. Sometimes the best solutions come from ideas that initially sound crazy. In addition, there is a natural tendency for the scribe to change proposals into his or her own words before writing on the flip. Often the interpretation is not what was meant, so ensure what is written is what was actually said.

4   Try to encourage a relaxed, friendly and productive atmosphere. By 'relaxed' we mean that people feel able to propose anything. In fact, encourage 'zany' ideas. There is nothing wrong with a bit of fun as long as the group are laughing with the person and not at them!

When the chair and group feel that all the ideas have been exhausted, the criteria can be set. Use the essentials to eliminate any unworkable options.

From this point forward, the structure is the same as for logical decisions.

Structure for 'creative' decisions
- Cover the purpose, i.e. generate options
- Set the ground rules
  - quantity rather than quality is important (at this stage)
  - do not set criteria yet; ensure people understand that they should not evaluate ideas and why
  - all ideas are to be recorded verbatim
- encourage a relaxed, friendly and productive atmosphere
- when the ideas have been generated, set the criteria and use the essentials to eliminate any unworkable options
- then return to the structure for 'logical' decisions

Planning or reviewing progress

Many meetings include objectives to plan some activity or to review progress against a plan produced at an earlier meeting.

Structure for producing a plan
1 *Clarify the objective to which the plan relates.* Ensure that it is clear, realistic, measurable, and result-oriented, and that it includes any constraints and a deadline.

2 *Identify what needs to be done* to meet the objective, i.e. decide what are the *key tasks*.

3 *Consider the resources required* to meet the objective alongside those actually available.

4 *Decide who should be responsible* for ensuring that each key task is completed on time and to the right standard.

5 Finally, *decide by when each key task must be completed* to meet the overall deadline.

Structure for reviewing progress
Often these sessions are too 'backward-looking'. The past is gone; we can really only learn from it and react accordingly. Most people do not find it difficult to plan; making the plan actually work is a different matter! While, for control purposes, it is important to review actual progress to date, it is also important to look *ahead*, and try to prevent future difficulties. This increases the chances of success.

1 Review *what should have happened* by this point.

2 Review *what has actually happened*, together with reasons for any differences, and more importantly, *what has already been done about them to put the plan back on track.*

3 Look ahead, identify any major *potential difficulties* and collectively decide what can be done to *eliminate the causes* or, at least, *reduce the effect* if the difficulty arises.

4 Decide *what further action is needed*, by whom and by when, and get *commitment* from the people concerned to those actions and deadlines.

Solving problems

Some people seem to combine problem-solving with decision-making, seeing them as part and parcel of the same thing. We believe that it is more helpful to separate them as the purpose and structure are different.

What is 'problem-solving'?
We see problem-solving as identifying the unknown cause(s) of something that is 'off-track', i.e. we don't know why have sales of a particular product fallen in Branch 'X' only.

What is the structure for problem-solving in a meeting?
Basically, there are three main steps:

- define the problem
- identify the possible causes
- decide which cause is producing the problem

1 *Define the problem* As Sherlock Holmes said: *'It is a capital mistake to theorise before one has data.'* This step in the structure is concerned with collecting this data.

We think that Rudyard Kipling's 'six honest serving men' help here:

> 'I keep six honest serving men, (they taught me all I knew); Their names are What and Why and When, and How and Where and Who.'

'Why' is the whole point of problem-solving. That is what we are trying to find out. Use the other five to collect the data.

2 *Identify possible causes of the problem* Newton's First Law of Motion (simplified) says that 'unless acted upon by force, a body will continue at the same speed and in a straight line'. For a problem to arise, there has to be a change, i.e. a force has to be applied.

Ask the group to *identify the changes that have taken place* which are relevant to the problem.

Now, *identify possible causes from those changes*: for example, a number of new sales staff might have been recruited in Branch X immediately prior to the problem of falling sales, so a possible cause might be 'lower sales due to inexperienced sales staff'.

3 *Decide which cause is producing the problem* Look at each possible cause and check it against the 'what, where, when, who, how' data collected earlier. Follow the Sherlock Holmes principle: 'When you have eliminated the impossible, whatever remains, however improbable, must be the truth'.

Communicating information

The type and complexity of information varies enormously and it may be communicated by the chair or by one or more of the participants. Whoever is involved in passing on the information, the major principle here is that the chair must ensure that the information is *understood*!

The broad structure should be:

1 Explain the objective and background, *stressing why the information is important to the group.*

2 Briefly outline what will be covered (so people know what to expect and how long it will take).

3 Communicate the information as clearly and concisely as possible:

- keep it short and simple
- use visual means where possible
- encourage questions for clarification
- avoid irrelevant 'side-tracking'

4 Summarise the key points that people must remember/ act upon and, again, check that they *understand* by encouraging questions from the group.

Checking reactions

Occasionally, the chair or one of the attendees may want to check reactions to a proposal before the final decision is made by the proposer or perhaps someone not even at the meeting.

A major trap can arise here. The proposer appreciates that he or she is simply *consulting* the group, but fails to make that clear (or purposely avoids doing so). As a result, the group believe that they are collectively being asked to *make the decision*. If the subsequent decision is not what the group expected then it is quite likely that there will be adverse reaction.

An effective structure here is vital:

1   Explain the objective and background as usual.

2   Ensure that the group realise that they are being *consulted*, and *explain* why that is.

3   Outline the proposal, and ask for their views; recording their views briefly on a flip chart will show that the proposer is listening.

4   Thank the group for their input, explain what happens next, and when the group will be told of the outcome.

If, when subsequently feeding-back the outcome to the group, the final decision ran contrary to their views, it is important to explain why that was. When looking at the overall picture, the decision-maker might take a decision that gives significant benefits to one part of the business but accepts that there will be some less significant snags in another department because of it. Often people only seem to see (or are only told) things that affect them and their own department.

An example of this might help. In a manufacturing firm some time ago now, the Board made a decision (after consulting the Production Manager and Foreman) to accept a very lucrative (but extremely difficult) contract for which the Sales Department had been invited to quote. The contract had very tight deadlines and so caused a whole host of production scheduling difficulties. The contract was completed on time, but you can probably imagine the comments from the folk in Production, most directed against Sales!

Sadly, nobody had explained that the contract had significantly increased the turnover/profit which would benefit everyone. This was only communicated *after the bad feeling had arisen*.

Summary

'Logical' decisions
- use a flip chart to help in reducing cross-table argument
- set criteria before reviewing options
- cover snags as well as benefits

'Creative' decisions
- explain ground rules for generating options
- quantity not quality
- do not set criteria yet (no evaluation)
- record all ideas verbatim
- relaxed, friendly, productive atmosphere

Planning
- use 'what, who, and by when' format

Reviewing progress
- remember to look ahead and try to identify major difficulties; try to eliminate the causes or reduce the effect

Solving problems
- define the problem – what, where, when, who, how (Kipling)
- identify possible causes – problems result from changes (remember Newton's Law)
- decide the cause(s) – eliminate the impossible (Sherlock Holmes)

Communicating information
- ensure that they know why it is important
- make sure they actually understand it

Checking reactions
- ensure that the participants understand the objective and their role
- don't let them confuse consultation with joint decision-making

Control: handling difficult participants

Years ago, most meetings tended to be very 'formal' with everyone speaking 'through the chair' and people addressing each other as 'Mr', 'Mrs' or 'Miss'. Now, meetings generally operate on a more informal basis with cross-table discussion encouraged and most people using first names. This 'free-ranging' approach can make the process of controlling the input quite difficult for the chair.

Most participants at most meetings are constructive and will do their best to help the chair and others at the meeting to achieve a result. So, in looking at how to handle difficult participants, we are invariably looking at a small percentage of meeting attendees. The problem is that they can take a disproportionate amount of the chair's time and they have to be controlled effectively if the objectives are to be achieved.

Think about a regular meeting that you attend or chair, identify any 'difficult' participants, and consider how they are handled.

There are many 'names' we can attach to these difficult participants (and probably so can you!). Rather than try to identify ways of handling every type of difficult participant, we decided to use the 80/20 rule and concentrate on the 20% that cause 80% of the difficulties.

The main classifications of difficult participants we identified are:

- the perennial latecomer
- the talkative person
- the quiet (uninvolved) person
- the joker
- the person who blocks new ideas or change
- the aggressive person, who 'attacks' people

Before looking at how to handle these people *reactively*, it is worth repeating that prevention is better than cure.

- a clear, objective-based agenda can reduce the chances of confusion
- explaining the roles of the participants should help them to contribute effectively
- setting ground rules should indicate how the chair expects participants to behave

However, with the best will in the world, we can't prevent every possibly disruptive input! To handle difficult participants, we need to be able to do two things: clearly identify the difficult behaviour, then handle that behaviour as quickly and effectively as possible.

The ideas that follow depend on participants recognising the authority of the chair, and responding to direction from the chair. Special problems can occur for the chair when the difficult participant is very senior, or from another organisation. The chair often feels in 'Catch 22' in these cases. Good old common sense says that these people need to be handled differently, and this will be covered on Friday.

For each of the 'classifications', e.g. latecomers, we have tried to define what we mean by the title and then suggest actions that can be taken by the chair to control the input.

The perennial latecomer

This is the person who consistently arrives five or more minutes late.

In the sample agenda on Monday, (*sharp please!*) was put after the start time. If you use this phrase, you must be prepared to actually to *do* it. So what happens if, despite this, there *is* a latecomer?

Think about the meetings that you attend or run. The most common reaction is for the chair to summarise proceedings so far and then carry on. A summary is fair when the lateness was genuinely unavoidable, but often lateness is avoidable. Everyone is busy but the other participants

RUSH, RUSH RUSH!

managed to arrive on time. If the chair immediately summarises, what has the latecomer learned? 'If I arrive late, I have saved some time and have not really lost anything.'

How to handle
Consider using one of the alternative approaches. *Halt* the entire meeting and watch the latecomer intently while they sit and sort out their papers. Alternatively, *ignore* the latecomer (apart from 'hello') *for about five minutes*. You 'owe' the people who took the trouble to arrive on time, so why disrupt the meeting with a summary? During this short period the latecomer will feel uncomfortable, but they are very unlikely to be late again!

The talkative person

This is the person who takes up too much of the 'air-time', (known lovingly to friends as 'Megamouth'); *not* the person who is doing most of the talking because they have all the information or have been asked by the group for their ideas.

The talkative person can be positive or negative. The trap is over-control by the chair. 'He's off again so I must stop him now.' While he or she may use 300 words where 30 would do, we often get many useful ideas (suggestions or reasoned disagreements) from them, so we don't want to cut them off unreasonably and thereby lose their ideas.

How to handle
Interrupting someone who is trying to help is hard, but there are ways of doing it without offence – primarily by using their name. Names are important to us and we tend to respond when we hear ours. Have you ever heard someone say your name at the other side of a crowded room?

Allow them their (reasonable) say as long as they are on the point, then summarise the key points they have made, thank them, and *immediately* move the discussion on to someone else. 'Fred, from what you have said, you are enthusiastic about the idea because, primarily, it will give us considerable savings. Thanks for that. Jane, what do you think about it?'

If they keep interrupting, remind them of the ground rules (assuming that you set some): 'John, remember that I asked all of you to let everyone put their suggestions, then we would discuss them. Please let Diane finish, then I will come back to you.'

The quiet (uninvolved) person

This is the person who says virtually nothing, when you would expect them to be contributing.

There are two main causes for this:

> • the person may feel 'out of their depth', e.g. a new member of the team at their first meeting, or someone relatively junior at a senior management meeting
> • the person may feel that they have no interest in this part of the meeting

How to handle

The most common, and *worst*, thing to say to the person who feels out of their depth is: 'Marion, you have been quiet. What do you think?' They are already feeling awkward and this will probably make them wish for the floor to open up and swallow them.

They are there for a reason, and it is important to cover this at the start of the meeting. e.g: 'Marion has forgotten more about computers than most of us will ever know, so I have asked her to help us today.' This may well give them the confidence they need to contribute.

If they are still quiet or uncertain, give them some thinking time but encourage input, e.g: 'Marion, after we have heard from Jim, I would like your view on which computer would suit our needs. You know the models better than us.'

One cautionary note: Please try to remember to *go back to them*. It is all too easy to forget and they are unlikely to speak until invited.

The *person who has no interest* requires different handling. This will become quite apparent in their responses to questions:

Chair: 'What do you think, David?'

David: 'Doesn't really matter what I think. It doesn't affect me.'

The first point is that there must be a way in which David is affected, otherwise why is he there? It may be that he didn't realise that this issue *will* affect him (next month, perhaps, if not now). In these cases, explain why the person has been invited, then again allow them some thinking time.

What if it is not clear *why* there is a lack of interest? It may sound like stating the obvious to say that a bit of probing is needed. Strangely enough, the disinterested person is often ignored, provided that they are not causing disruption. Try to find out *why* they have no interest, and deal with the concern if possible:

Chair: 'What do you think, David?'

David: 'Doesn't matter. Nothing ever changes'.

Chair: 'Why do you say nothing changes?'

David: 'We discussed this at a meeting before you came. We just talked, nothing was decided. It was pointless.'

Chair: 'Going back to our objective for this, I intend us to *make* a decision today and implement it so things *will* change. Does that help?' etc.

The joker

This the person who seems to make light of everything and overdoes the humour.

It may just stem from a natural sense of humour, or it may be a way of releasing a bit of tension in a difficult situation. There is no law that states that meetings have to be serious all of the time to achieve something. Humour in the right situation can be a real advantage, providing it is not overdone.

How to handle
If it 'oils the wheels' of the meeting and is in small doses, allow it; it's a benefit!

If it is inappropriate or overdone, explain how you feel, and why, then ask the person to give you a suggestion or reaction *relevant* to the issue under discussion. This will get the conversation back on track.

The person who blocks new ideas or change

This is the person who objects to ideas or change *without giving reasons*, e.g.: 'We have tried that before. It won't work'.

It is important not to confuse them with someone who is disagreeing, i.e. giving reasons for their objection to an idea. For example: 'We don't have enough cash in the budget so I don't think we can do that.' Disagreement is often helpful in arriving at a workable solution as it frequently leads to progress. In this example, the meeting may well move on to finding ways of reducing the cost of the proposal or finding extra money to supplement the existing budget.

How to handle
The most common trap is to *ignore* the blocker and concentrate on the positive people. The result is that they can continue to block and this will very quickly 'kill' any positive atmosphere.

The best approach, in the face of a block, is the 'spotlight' principle. Stop the meeting and ask the blocker why they feel the idea is no good, will not work, etc. and then try, if possible, to get a positive action or solution from them, e.g.:

Bertie the Block: 'I disagree!' (That's the classic block.)

Chair: 'Bertie, why do you disagree?'

Bertie: 'Well, it just won't work'

Chair: 'Why?'

Bertie: 'Far too expensive'

Chair: 'Can you think of a way of making it cheaper then?' etc.

There will often be pauses before 'Bertie' answers. We don't like pauses. The constructive people will often try to help but *ensure that the 'spotlight' remains firmly on 'Bertie'*, without upsetting the positive people.

The aggressive person

This is the person who launches personal attacks at other people in the meeting e.g.; 'Pat, that's a stupid idea. Use some common sense for once.'

We are *not* using the word 'aggressive' here as it is often applied to salespeople to indicate someone who is rather 'pushy', nor should it be confused with hard disagreement, e.g.: 'Absolutely not, Pat. There is no way we can afford to do this now.'

How to handle
In the face of an attack, people often respond in like manner. This can quickly develop into a full-scale row that will badly affect or even destroy the meeting. The chair needs to act very quickly here and *stop it* before it develops. Very firm control is needed. The person needs to be told that attacks are unacceptable, but disagreement is valid, e.g.: 'Mark, hold it! Pat put forward a proposal that you obviously dislike. Having a go at her doesn't help. Please keep to the issue rather than attack Pat.' If, despite this, the person still persists with the attacks, try calling a coffee break and have a private word with them. They need to understand the difference between attacks and disagreement, and behave appropriately.

What if the difficult person continues to be difficult?

The preceding ideas are all reactions to various forms of difficult behaviour, aimed at minimising the effect. To change behaviour, we need to find out why the person *keeps doing it*, i.e. find the real *cause(s)*. This is often too time consuming or too sensitive to do in the meeting so it needs a separate, *private* discussion with the person afterwards.

The aim is to find out why the person keeps behaving in this way at the meeting, and then *jointly* to agree an approach that will remove the difficult behaviour.

Ask them for suggestions rather than propose your own ideas. They are more likely to be committed to their own ideas.

It will help to concentrate on the actual behaviour, rather than appear to be attacking the person:

'Four ideas were put forward and you objected to all of them without giving any reasons. Why?'

as opposed to:

'Why were you so incredibly negative?' (even though that may be what you *want* to say!)

Summary

Handling difficult participants
- Latecomer: if lateness unjustified, ignore them for five minutes
- Talkative: allow them their say, summarise, and move the discussion to someone else
- Quiet (out of their depth): explain their expertise, allow them 'thinking time'
- Quiet (uninterested): find out why; explain relevance to them
- Joker: explain how you feel; ask for a relevant suggestion to get back on track
- Blocker: 'spotlight', probe for the reason, try to get a constructive suggestion
- Aggressive: stop it quickly, give a firm explanation of the rules; if persistent, call a coffee break and talk privately

Control: some further challenges

Yesterday we looked at a specific aspect of controlling the meeting that most chairs find hard: handling difficult participants. Today we will look at more general issues around controlling the meeting:

- handling more senior people
- handling people from other organisations
- chairing 'from the back'
- ensuring that results are achieved:
  - the importance of summaries
  - why visibility is so important

Most managers feel reasonably comfortable about running meetings involving their own team of people. They know everybody and there is built-in 'authority' because the chair is also the manager. Controlling the meeting becomes far more difficult when more senior managers or people from another department or organisation attend.

Some fairly common questions that we are asked on courses include:

- 'How can I stop my boss from taking over?'
- 'The chairing of one of the meetings I attend is terrible. How can I make it more productive without upsetting the chair?'
- 'How do I ensure that the output is clear to everyone?'

Handling more senior people

As mentioned on Sunday, having a senior manager at the meeting can be a distinct advantage, but sometimes they tend to take over! They are often used to running meetings, so fall naturally into the role of 'chair'. This is compounded by the fact that people often address their comments to the most senior person there.

Some senior managers are well aware of this reaction, clearly state that they are a 'guest' at the meeting and recognise, as any other participant, the role of the chair. Obviously, there is no problem for the chair in these cases.

However, life is not usually quite that simple. If you need to invite a senior manager to your meeting but anticipate difficulties, what should you do?

Preventing difficulties

The best way to handle difficulties is to *prevent* them from arising. The best way to describe how difficulties with senior managers might be prevented in future is to work through what we believe is a fairly typical situation. Let's say that the chair, John, ran a team meeting that was attended by his boss, Shirley. As she was the most senior person there, people understandably tended to address the questions to her and the input from her took the meeting off-track.

Later, Shirley introduced an issue that was not on the agenda. John wasn't sure whether to allow discussion to continue or not, because the spare time he had included had already been used up. He decided that 'discretion was the better part of valour', so the meeting ran well over the planned finish time.

Does this sound at all familiar?

Now poor old John has a real dilemma. Assuming that Shirley's input is required at future meetings, does he discuss the problem with her and risk upsetting Shirley, or accept the situation and try to handle it as it occurs, with the risk that the meeting slips out of *his* control, as chair?

Our view is: discuss the potential difficulties with the senior manager *privately*, and *before the next meeting*.

Most managers will be prepared to discuss your concerns in private and will want to help, providing that you are constructive. They probably chair and perhaps didn't realise just what they did.

Situations and people differ widely, of course, so there is no, one right way! However, if you decide that your situation/

relationships are appropriate and believe this approach is worth a try, here are a few guidelines.

A positive, constructive approach (rather than a complaint) by the chair should reduce the risk of upset. Before any discussion, remember to consider the benefits of the senior person's attendance as well as the difficulties. Think about how those difficulties might be prevented at future meetings without losing the benefit of their input, and decide your objective for the discussion.

Returning to the example, in the private discussion with Shirley, John would probably start by covering the purpose of this discussion, and the benefits of Shirley's input to the previous meeting. He would then move on to the issues around 'side-tracking', the additional agenda item, and time control. The idea is to be tactful, but honest! John could either suggest possible actions for the next meeting, or ask Shirley for her ideas.

The outcome of such a meeting might include agreement that:

- John will plan specific time for Shirley to answer questions from the team
- Shirley will notify John of any additional objectives for the meeting (with an estimated time) so the agenda can be modified in advance

Handling difficulties during the meeting
Suppose, for whatever reason, you cannot prevent difficulties (on this occasion), and they arise. What do you actually do?

First, *tact* is vital! Nobody will gain if the meeting degenerates into an argument between the chair and a senior manager over 'control'.

- gently, remind *everyone* of the objectives and ground rules for the meeting
- ensure that you respect their *role*, even though you may disagree with their *views*. Every senior manager occasionally has to 'quote the company line', even though they might personally disagree with it, but are unable to change it.
- use 'we' and not 'you' when trying to control. '*We* are taking too long on this' is very different from '*You* are taking too long on this'

If you are having real difficulty, call a coffee break and try to have a 'quiet' discussion with the senior person. Try to find a benefit for them in behaving in the way you wish e.g. 'Ken, I need your help. I know Project X is important to you but if we spend too long on it, we won't have any time left to finalise the budget that you need.'

Handling people from other organisations

Have you ever found yourself in a situation where you have a perfectly clear agenda for your meeting and someone from outside comes in and wants to change the whole thing?

To try to suggest ideas to cover every situation where there may be 'outsiders' in a meeting would be impossible. However, there are a few general points that might help.

Once again, *tact* is vital! Consider sending them an advance copy of the agenda (titled '*Suggested* Agenda') and invite them to propose any changes or additions they feel appropriate. Invariably, there will be few or no changes! People seem to find the agenda clear and, because it says 'suggested' and they have the option to change it, do not seem to feel that they have been railroaded.

You could also phone or, if sufficiently important, even go and see them if it helps to prevent potential difficulties. Finally, at the start of the meeting, verify agreement to your agenda and any ground rules, then control as you would with a senior manager

Chairing 'from the back'

As with everything some 'chairs' are better than others! There can be few things more frustrating than for someone who has a pretty good idea of how to chair than to sit through a badly chaired meeting. As a participant, you want the meeting to achieve a positive result but fear that the 'chair' will not make that happen. The answer? Chair it 'from the back'.

Chairing 'from the back' is exercising some control over the meeting (without taking over) when you are not the chair.

This whole approach hinges on one very important principle; the idea is to *help* the ineffective 'chair', rather than challenge his or her authority. The chair may well realise that things are not going as well as they should and a direct challenge to their authority as chair is only likely to make matters worse. So, how do you do it?

How to chair 'from the back'

- be tactful (even though you may not feel like it)
- use questions, aimed at the 'chair'

Tact is vital if you are to avoid the impression of challenging the chair's ability to run the meeting. 'For Heaven's sake get a grip on this meeting, Chair! Harry's rambling again,' really won't help much.

The idea is to 'guide' the chair via questions, rather than make procedural proposals as you would if you were chairing. Turn the procedural proposal into a question, and address it to the 'chair'.

For example, let's say that one agenda item is finished and the meeting is about to move onto the next, without any summary. In a meeting where you are the chair, you might say something like: 'Let's just summarise the actions we have agreed.' In this meeting, you realise that a summary is vital for clarity and the chair is not going to 'oblige', so you might say: 'Paul [the chair], before we move on, could we have a summary, please, as I'm not too sure who is doing what?' This approach *prompts* the chair but still leaves them 'in control', as it is the chair who decides.

Here are a few more examples:

Procedural suggestion you might make as chair	Question to the chair 'from the back'
'We need to identify what needs to be done, who should do it, and by when.'	'Ken, would it help us to list on the flip chart what needs to be done, etc.'

'We have looked at the benefits of that option. Let's look at any snags before we decide.'

'Jane, before we make the decision, would it be worth just identifying any snags?'

'We have moved away from the original objective and need to get back to it.'

'Ron, could you just remind me of our objective for this, please?'

Phrase the wording of the questions to suit your own approach. It is the principle that is important.

Ensuring that results are achieved

One of the most frequent criticisms of meetings goes something like: 'All we did was "discuss". Nothing was achieved!' In the last section today, we will look at ways to help ensure that results *are* achieved, and, what's more, are apparent to everyone there.

There are five main areas to consider:

- the importance of summaries
- why visibility is so important
- producing 'minutes'
- getting commitment to actions
- following up after the meeting

The first two will be considered here, the remaining three in the next chapter.

The importance of summaries

An effective summary by the chair does two very important things:

> • it ensures that what has been agreed is understood by all concerned
> • it clearly identifies the result that has been achieved

On Wednesday, when we looked at a structure for communicating information, we stressed the importance of ensuring that people actually *understood* the information. The same principle holds true here. Even the best-run meetings contain a bit of 'multi-speak' occasionally. Some key decision might be made during the course of the discussion, but one or more of the group might simply not hear it, or misinterpret it. The summary at the end of each item (objective) on the agenda reduces the chances of a key factor being missed, or misinterpreted. Even the best chair can make mistakes, so the summary also enables the group to correct any errors by the chair.

Rather like a scoreboard at a football match, an effective summary also identifies the specific result that has been achieved, and makes this apparent to everyone there.

This is done by linking back to the objective for that part of the agenda, e.g: 'Our objective here was to decide which personal computer to buy. We have decided that it will be the XYZ model, purchased by Jim, and installed by the end of next month'.

What should the summary contain?

- *start* by saying something like 'Right, let's summarise'
  It is important that your summary is *heard*! Telling the group what is coming next gets their attention directed at you
- *the result, linked to the objective*: remind the group of the objective, and state the result that has been achieved as we did in the example above.
- *key points from the discussion*: the important word here is 'key'. Don't try to repeat everything! Ask yourself what the group must remember from that part of the meeting, e.g. why a particular option was chosen
- *any action plan* (what, who and by when): if you have used a flip chart, this should already be recorded, but you might want to stress any key factors, e.g. the importance of meeting the various deadlines
- check that your summary is *correct*: nobody is perfect and any mistakes are fairly easy to rectify at this stage

Why visibility is so important
As we have said in earlier chapters, visibility is important for clarity.

Think about a meeting where there were no visual aids and notes were taken by a 'minute secretary'. Have you, as a participant, made any important point and then wondered if the 'secretary' actually noted it?

If a scribe uses a flip chart or 'wipe-clean' board, or writes on an overhead transparency, people can actually *see* that their point has been noted. They do not have to waste time wondering if it has been registered. In addition, the information is visible to everyone throughout that phase of the discussion so they don't have to try to remember what was said.

Objective: (from the agenda)

Result: (e.g. the decision made)

What: (key tasks)   **Who?**   **By When?**

Issues to be resolved   **Deadline for reply**

Most meeting objectives result in some form of action plan, we have reproduced above a format which suits most situations.

The last section 'Issues to be resolved', is used to record any questions that cannot be resolved during the meeting, together with the date by which the answer must be obtained.

As we mentioned on Monday, some people have reservations about using visual aids in this way as they feel them to be a bit schoolteacherish. The scribe is not 'teaching'; he or she is trying to record accurately the views of the meeting and the results. We firmly believe that the benefits far outweigh the snags, so all we can really say is 'Try it'. We have never found anyone who actually objected to the use of a flip, though the scribe or chair must be prepared for the odd 'light-hearted insult' if it has not been tried before. People very soon see the benefits, and some chairs (or groups) even *insist* on the use of a flip chart or similar facility.

Summary

Handling more senior people
- discuss potential problems beforehand in private
- in the meeting, be tactful. Remind everyone of the ground rules. Use 'we', not 'you'

Handling people from other organisations
- tact again!
- send them a 'suggested agenda' well in advance
- at the start of the meeting, verify agreement to the agenda and ground rules

Chairing 'from the back'
- the aim is to help, not challenge
- turn procedural proposals into questions addressed to the chair

Ensuring that results are achieved
- summaries are vital for clarification and to identify clearly the result achieved
- use a flip chart (or similar) to record information and results to make them clearly visible to all

Ensuring that results are achieved

Yesterday we started to deal with controlling the meeting to ensure that results are achieved, covering the importance of summaries and why visibility is so important.

Today we will deal with the remaining aspects of control to ensure that results are achieved:

- producing minutes
- getting commitment to action
- following up on progress/commitments after the meeting

The processes of clarifying what is to be recorded in the minutes and getting commitment to the actions very often run together in the meeting. For clarity, we have separated the two.

...OUR ACE
MINUTE-TAKER

Producing minutes

Have you ever received a set of minutes a few days after a meeting, read through them, and thought to yourself, 'I don't know which meeting *you* attended but I don't think it was the same one that I attended!'?

Occasionally, the minutes do not seem to bear any resemblance to what the participants *believed* was actually agreed. We all know that effective communication is hard at the best of times. Too often, we are all guilty of misinterpretation. We don't mean to do it, it just happens.

What are minutes?
They should be an accurate record of proceedings.

In our opinion, the minutes should always relate to the specific objective(s) for the meeting. For example, if the objective was to make a decision from a set number of options, our minutes would show the objective, list the options, show what the decision was, and why it was chosen.

The amount of detail can range from a complete verbatim record (very rare nowadays), through key points raised in the discussions, to brief notes of the decisions made or action plans produced.

Deciding how much detail to record

The best way of deciding this is to set the criteria for minutes, i.e. what purpose must they serve, then agree the appropriate level of detail with the group.

The principle that we use is to record the minimum amount of detail necessary to achieve that purpose, and precede any record with a summary.

This saves time and should reduce the chances of misunderstanding. The production of 'formal' minutes has already been well documented, so we will concentrate on a more informal approach, which we call 'action minutes'.

'Action minutes'

Think about a situation where the minutes of a meeting that you attended arrive on your desk. What do you first look for?

Probably, a quick scan for your initials, the action you must take, and the deadline. Are we right?

Wherever possible, we use what we term 'action minutes' that concentrate on the things that people really want to know: the *results* (what decisions were made and why, what actions were agreed etc.).

If, as we have suggested before, you use a flip chart (or similar) in your meeting, you already have the basis for 'action minutes'. It may well be possible simply to pass the flips as they stand to whoever will type the minutes; or you may need to add one or two additional paragraphs to elaborate on the contents of the flip, in order to meet the criteria of the minutes that were agreed with the group.

Look back at our action plan described in 'Why visibility is so important' on Friday. Ask yourself if information in that format would be adequate as minutes? Would it meet the criteria you have set for the minutes? While this level of detail will not be sufficient for every type of meeting, all we can really say is that most people seem to like it!

Most 'chairs' try to send out the minutes as soon as possible after the meeting. If you are fortunate enough to have one of those flip charts with an A4 copier attached which copies the contents of the flip, people might be happy just to have the copy as minutes. There is no delay time and the typist will probably thank you as well.

Getting commitment to actions

What is 'commitment'?
In the context of meetings, we define 'commitment' as specific agreement to take responsibility for the action (and result), whether acting personally or choosing to involve someone else.

Why is it needed?
All too often some 'chairs' assume (or like to assume) that they have commitment when they do not!

Have you ever heard someone say, when they receive the minutes, 'I didn't agree to do that'? It might be a simple misunderstanding, but often it is caused by the 'chair' actually failing to check for commitment. The thinking goes something like: 'Fred hasn't said "No" so that's OK.'

There are several 'warning signs' that *might* indicate a lack of commitment:

- total silence, i.e. a complete lack of reaction (to their initials on the plan, or being mentioned by name in the summary)
- negative reactions:
  - 'I'll try.' 'Try' might not be good enough!
  - 'I suppose so, but why me?'
  - 'Yes, but' the phrase that follows 'but' often doesn't get heard, or it is ignored.

You can probably identify others from your own experiences.

So how do you actually go about getting this 'specific agreement', then?

How do you get commitment to action?
As we have mentioned before, the chances of commitment are likely to be higher if you involve the people in the decision, plan, etc.

However, not everyone actually wants to take responsibility!

Have you ever heard anyone use the following excuse for not acting?

'Ah, but I didn't actually *say* that I would do that!'

A course delegate told us recently of a standing rule in the meetings in their organisation. There is a poster in each meeting room that states the rules for all meetings, including: 'Silence will be taken as agreement!'

It is a good idea; but we still believe it is important actually to check for commitment!

This might seem like stating the obvious, but *ask them* – 'David, are you happy to arrange for the computer to be delivered by 30th October?' or whatever words suit your style. Sadly, there are some 'chairs' around who just never seem to ask this type of question – *ever*!

Then, wait for them to reply! Remember that you are checking for 'specific agreement'; an incoherent grunt will not do. We believe that a 'public' verbal commitment will increase the likelihood of the action being taken.

Following up on progress/commitments after the meeting

Why is follow up needed?
Some meetings spend the first 15 or 30 minutes bemoaning the fact that actions should have been taken but, for a whole host of reasons, have not been. In short, nothing has actually been achieved since the last meeting. That is why some form of follow-up is needed!

Who should do the follow up?
Assuming that you agree follow-up is necessary, the next question is: 'who should do it?' Someone has to do it, and we believe that it should be the 'chair'.

In fairness, some people feel that follow-up is outside the role of the 'chair' and that their responsibilities end when the meeting ends (apart from producing the minutes). It is then up to the individuals to take the actions to which they have agreed.

We view follow-up as an important part of the overall 'result-oriented' approach to meetings. The result often doesn't actually materialise until something has been *done*! For example, the meeting might produce a decision to buy a computer, but the real 'result' is not achieved until the computer is actually installed.

While the 'chair' might not have the authority to *demand* action, he or she can often '*prompt*' it, if necessary, because of the commitments made in the original meeting.

If in doubt, ask the group to decide in the meeting what should be done regarding follow up.

What should be monitored?

- *critical tasks*, i.e. those which are vital for the achievement of the overall result, for example, the preparation of a key presentation to the Board by a certain date.
- *tasks on which other tasks depend*, e.g. producing a summary of the last twelve months' actual expenditure so that a budget for next year can be produced at the next meeting

Who should be monitored?

I'M SO GLAD YOU'RE PERSUADED—I HATE HAVING TO USE THIS STUFF

We all know that some people always 'deliver', others simply do not! Ensure that you follow up on those who need it.

When to follow up?
The key point here is to follow up in time to prevent difficulties at the next meeting. Suppose an action has to be taken before the next meeting (on 30 November) and it is now 1 November. A follow up on 15 November will still allow two weeks if problems are apparent.

Minutes (including the action plans) can often get filed in a 'bring-forward' file awaiting the next meeting, so missed deadlines don't become apparent until too late. A small tip: note follow up reminders *in your diary* on the date concerned, e.g.: 'phone Ted re installation of the computer.'

How should you follow up?

- ask how things are going to check whether progress is 'on track'
- if 'off track', identify why, and what can be done to get things back 'on track'. Consider whether it is appropriate for you to offer help
- consider what you, as 'chair', might do in future meetings to prevent similar difficulties occurring again

One final point regarding follow-up
While not strictly follow-up in the sense we have used it, consider a 'follow-up' *on yourself* after the meeting.

If you chair meetings now, ask yourself whether you evaluate your own performance after a meeting? Often what happens is this: if the meeting went wrong, people will spend a considerable amount of time trying to evaluate what (or who!) caused the problem and deciding what can be done to prevent a similar situation in the future. That's fine. We *should* look for ways to improve our meetings; but what about the 'other side of the coin'? What do you do if the meeting goes well?

Most 'chairs' that we have encountered say something like, 'That was a good meeting' or, 'That went better than I expected', and simply move on to the next task on their list. Always try to spend some time as soon as possible after the meeting to review two things:

- What went well, and why?
- What could have been improved, and how?

One 'chair' we know who is fairly new to running meetings actually asks the participants these questions at the end of his meetings. You might feel that it is not appropriate in the situations you face, but it is worth considering as he feels that he learns a great deal from this feedback.

Summary

Minutes
- decide purpose and level of detail with the group
- summarise before recording an item in the minutes
- consider using 'action minutes' to show the key results of the meeting

Getting commitment to action
- commitment is 'a specific agreement to take responsibility for the action (and result)'
- don't *assume* that you have commitment; actually *ask* the person if they agree to take the action, and wait for a reply

Following up after the meeting
- involve the group in deciding how follow-up should be handled
- monitor tasks that are critical for achievement of the overall result, and those tasks on which other tasks depend
- follow up in time to prevent a disaster
- if things have gone 'off track'; identify why, what can be done to put things back 'on track', and what can be done to prevent a recurrence in future meetings

What have you learned from reading this book?

Throughout the book you have probably compared your views on how meetings should be run with our thoughts. We hope that you have identified some useful ideas that you can use to improve the meetings in which you are involved.

While they are fresh in your mind, note them down in the space below, and, if possible, identify when you intend to implement them.

Useful idea	When to implement

Further *Successful Business in a Week* **titles from** Hodder & Stoughton and the Institute of Management all at £5.99

All Hodder & Stoughton books are available from your local bookshop or can be ordered direct from the publisher. Just tick the titles you want and fill in the form below. Prices and availability subject to change without notice.

To: Hodder & Stoughton Ltd, Cash Sales Department, Bookpoint, 39 Milton Park, Abingdon, Oxon, OX14 4TD. If you have a credit card you may order by telephone – 01235 831700.
Please enclose a cheque or postal order made payable to Bookpoint Ltd to the value of the cover price and allow the following for postage and packaging:
UK & BFPO: £1.00 for the first book, 50p for the second book and 30p for each additional book ordered up to a maximum charge of £3.00.
OVERSEAS & EIRE: £2.00 for the first book, £1.00 for the second book and 50p for each additional book.

Name:..

Address: ....

....

If you would prefer to pay by credit card, please complete:

Please debit my Visa/Mastercard/Diner's Card/American Express (delete as appropriate) card no:

❑ ❑ ❑ ❑ ❑ ❑ ❑ ❑ ❑ ❑ ❑ ❑ ❑ ❑ ❑ ❑

Signature .... Expiry Date ....

Conclusion

We all know how hard it is to chair a meeting really well. The perfect 'chair' has yet to be born, and no book will make him or her.

People and situations differ widely, so please remember that only you can decide when and how to apply the guidelines in this book.

What we do hope is that you have gained some ideas from reading this book that will help to make the meetings in which you are involved somewhat more effective.

We would like to thank all of the people (friends, colleagues and course delegates) over the years who have given us ideas and stories about good and bad meetings.

If, at some point in the future, you find yourself working with us on one of our courses, we will be delighted to see you and to discuss any aspects of this book with you.

We hope that you have enjoyed reading this book as much as we enjoyed writing it.

Thank you for buying it.